EGGS

Dorothy Turner

Illustrations by John Yates

Carolrhoda Books, Inc./Minneapolis

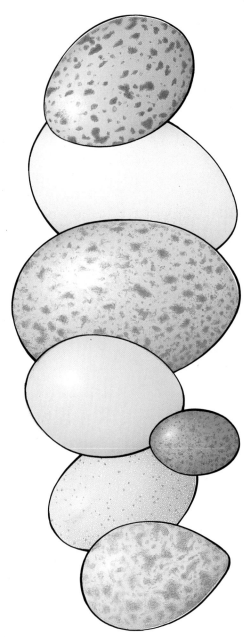

All words that appear in **bold** are
explained in the glossary on page 30.

First published in the U.S. in 1989 by
Carolrhoda Books, Inc.

LIBRARY OF CONGRESS
Library of Congress Cataloging-in-Publication Data

Turner, Dorothy
    Eggs / Dorothy Turner ; illustrated by John Yates.
      p.   cm.
    Bibliography: p.
    Includes index.
    Summary: Discusses how eggs are produced, cooked, and eaten, and
what role they play in various cultures.
    ISBN 0-87614-360-5 (lib. bdg.)
    1. Eggs as food—Juvenile literature. 2. Eggs—Juvenile
literature. 3. Cookery (Eggs)—Juvenile literature. [1. Eggs.
2. Cookery—Eggs.] I. Yates, John, ill. II. Title.
TX383.T87   1989
641.3'75—dc19   88-23631
                                                                      CIP
                                                                      AC

Printed in Italy by G. Canale C.S.p.A., Turin
Bound in the United States of America

1 2 3 4 5 6 7 8 9 10 99 98 97 96 95 94 93 92 91 90 89

Contents

Food for the world

hen

Eggs are an important food all over the world. In every country—from the icy lands near the North Pole to the hot countries near the equator— hens are kept for their eggs.

Most of the eggs we eat are hens' eggs, but those of other birds are also eaten. Many people in the Far East like to eat duck eggs. Goose eggs are popular in some parts of Europe.

duck

turtle

4

The eggs of quail, pigeons, gulls, pheasant, ostriches, and other birds are often eaten as a delicacy, a rare kind of food.

Not all the eggs we eat come from birds. Caviar is an expensive delicacy made from the eggs of a fish called a sturgeon. Even the eggs of reptiles such as turtles are sometimes eaten.

However, when we talk about eating eggs, we usually mean the hens' eggs that are sold all over the world. In this book, we will take a closer look at hens' eggs.

quail

goose

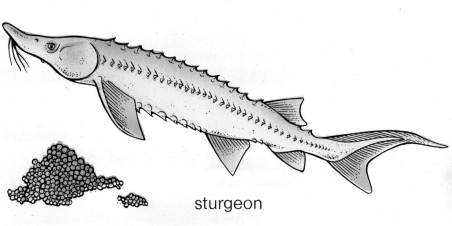

sturgeon

Eggs in the past

Thousands of years ago, people found out that some birds' eggs were good to eat. At first, people ate only eggs they picked up in the wild. Then they realized that if they tamed the birds, they could have eggs whenever they wanted.

The ancestors of our modern chickens were the wild jungle **fowl** of India. People in India learned how to tame these birds and collect their eggs. As early as four thousand years ago, the domesticated

Wild red jungle fowl in India. These were the first kind of chickens to be tamed.

Left: Ancient Egyptians carrying eggs and other food as offerings to their gods

Below: Rhode Island red hens scratching for food

fowl had spread from India to China, Japan, and Europe.

Much later, in 1493, the explorer Christopher Columbus took chickens with him on his second voyage to the New World. The hens' eggs were a valuable food for the sailors. This is how the first chickens were brought to America.

Today, farmers raise different kinds of chickens for different reasons—some for meat and some for egg laying. Two of the best-known kinds of chickens are leghorns and Rhode Island reds.

What eggs are like

The body of a female chicken (a hen) holds many tiny eggs. One by one, they grow and are laid. If an egg has been fertilized by a male bird (a rooster), a chick will grow inside it.

The drawings show what an egg looks like inside. You can see a yellow **yolk** surrounded by white (**albumen**), and an **air sac**. The spot on

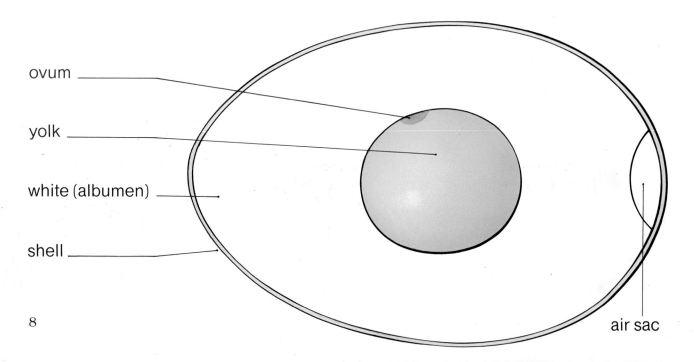

ovum

yolk

white (albumen)

shell

air sac

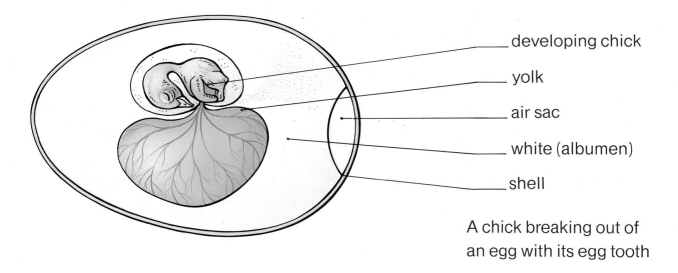

developing chick
yolk
air sac
white (albumen)
shell

A chick breaking out of an egg with its egg tooth

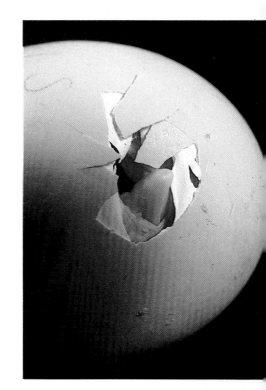

the yolk is the **ovum**, from which a new chick can grow in a **fertilized egg**.

As a tiny chicken grows inside an egg, it feeds on the yolk and albumen. It is protected by the shell around the egg. So an egg gives a chick both food and a home.

A mother hen sits on her eggs to keep them warm. After 21 days, a chick is ready to **hatch**. It begins to break the shell with its **egg tooth**, a sharp point on its beak. A chick may take a whole day to break out. Many birds, and some reptiles, get out of their eggs this way.

The food in an egg

An egg contains food for a growing chick. The eggs we buy to eat, however, do not have chicks growing in them. Those eggs have not been fertilized. Instead, we use the food ourselves.

The yolk and the white of an egg contain fat, **protein**, and **vitamins** and **minerals**. Fat gives us energy. Protein builds up our bodies. Vitamins and minerals help keep us healthy. About one-tenth of an egg is protein and about

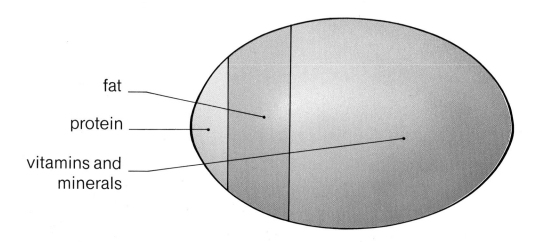

fat

protein

vitamins and
minerals

two-tenths is fat. The exact amount of vitamins and minerals in an egg depends on the kind of food a hen has been eating.

Eggs contain many nourishing substances. But egg yolks contain one substance, **cholesterol**, that can be bad for our health if we eat too much of it.

A boiled egg for breakfast is a tasty and nourishing way to start the day.

Egg farms

Chickens living in tightly packed cages on a poultry farm. The eggs are collected from a shelf below the cages.

Some egg farmers **mass-produce** eggs on different types of poultry farms. One type of farm has huge sheds where thousands of hens are kept tightly packed together in cages. The hens can't move around and never see daylight. They are simply egg-laying machines. Many people believe such farms are cruel, and they will not buy eggs produced there.

Another type of egg farming keeps chickens indoors but gives them some space and freedom of movement.

On another type of poultry farm, chickens are allowed to lead a natural life and can run around freely outdoors. The hens may lay their eggs in the open or in the shelter of a henhouse. They eat grass

Chickens living a
more natural life
on a small farm.
They are free to wander
around, feed, and lay
their eggs outdoors.

and insects and may be fed corn or scraps of
food. Chickens do not have teeth, so they can't
chew their food. They eat bits of shell and grit
that help to grind up the food in their stomachs
into small pieces.

From farm to store

A hen lays about 220 eggs a year, although some can produce an egg each day of the year! Young hens, called **pullets**, begin to lay eggs when they are about 5 or 6 months old. They continue to lay good eggs until they are about 18 months old. Then the pullets are killed, and their meat is used, often for pet food.

Eggs go from a farm to a central plant. There they are washed, sorted, and graded

Above: Eggs are passed over special lights to be checked for quality.

Right: These pullets are kept indoors in a warm barn. They lay their eggs in nest boxes.

14

Right: Eggs are sorted and graded before being packed in cartons.

Below: Most eggs end up in grocery stores, ready to be sold.

according to weight. Next, each egg is held in front of a light to check for quality. That way, the person checking the egg can see through the shell to the inside of the egg.

Eggs are packaged by size. Egg cartons are stamped with an **expiration date** and sent to grocery stores. Eggs that are not top quality are sometimes used by food companies to make cakes and cookies. Stale eggs, however, are always rejected.

Eggs are not just used for food. They are also used to make paint, ink, soap, shampoo, and fertilizers for plants.

Is this egg fresh?

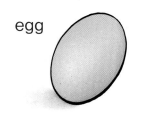

In this experiment, you can find out if an egg is fresh without breaking it open.

You will need:

an egg

1 teaspoon salt

water

a glass

salt

water

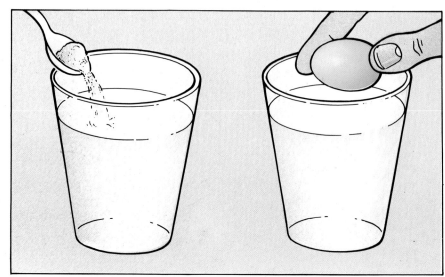

16

fresh

old

stale

1. Fill a glass with water, then stir in a teaspoon of salt.
2. Carefully add the egg.

If it lies at the bottom of the glass, the egg is fresh. If it floats to the surface, the egg is stale and shouldn't be used.

This test works because an old egg contains more air than a fresh egg, which makes the old egg float more easily.

The eggs we buy have been kept in cool storage. The longer an egg is stored, the more the egg white evaporates, or turns to vapor. As the white evaporates, the air sac at the top of the egg gets larger. That is why a stale egg floats in water.

You can also tell if an egg is fresh when you break it open. If the egg is fresh, the yolk will be firm and plump, and the white will be thick and jellylike. If the egg is stale, the yolk will be flat and thin, and the white will be watery. If the egg is very stale, it will smell horrible!

1.

Decorating eggs

A decorated egg is supposed to bring good luck. There are two ways to prepare an egg for decorating.

One way is to empty the eggshell by piercing each end of the egg with a needle and gently blowing out the contents. Another way is to leave the contents inside and hard-boil the egg. (See page 26 to find out how to hard-boil eggs.) Be sure to let the egg cool before decorating it.

1. To color an egg, you can buy paint or dye, or you can use vegetables. If you boil an egg with a beet, the shell will turn red; boiled with an onion skin, the shell will turn yellow. You can test different vegetables to get other colors.
2. Make a jeweled egg by gluing on sequins, cake decorations, or fake jewels.

3. Use paints or felt-tip pens to give your egg a face. Add cotton or yarn for hair. You could make a clown, or Santa Claus, or a picture of a friend.

4. Make a special gift for someone by writing a message on a painted egg.

You can make stands for your decorated eggs by cutting out individual cups from an egg carton.

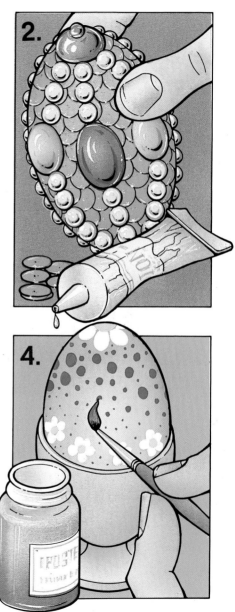

Beliefs about eggs

To people long ago, it must have seemed a miracle when an egg began to crack open and a tiny chick broke through the shell. It is not surprising, then, that eggs became important symbols of birth and creation.

One story of the creation of the world says the whole universe was born from an egg. This mythical egg is known as the world egg, or cosmic egg. An ancient Chinese story tells

A chick breaking its way out of an egg is an amazing sight. It has been the source of many stories about creation.

how the giant Pan Gu lay curled up in the egg that was the universe. When he broke out of the shell, the shattered pieces formed the earth and the heavens. Natives in Australia tell a story about the eagle and the emu, a large ostrichlike bird. In a rage, the eagle threw the emu's egg into the sky, and as it went up, the egg burst into flames and became the sun.

In countries of the Far East, eggs are specially wrapped and given as gifts at some weddings.

An Easter egg hunt
is a tradition
in many countries.

When we think of eggs, we often think of the
coming of spring and of new life. We think of the
birth of birds, plants, and animals. For
centuries, people have used eggs in fertility
rites. Some farmers still perform these ceremonies
each year to make their crops grow well and their
animals thrive and produce healthy young.

Because eggs remind us of new birth, in
the Christian religion, eggs are seen as symbols

of the rebirth of Christ, which is celebrated at Easter. This is why children give each other decorated eggs and candy eggs at Easter and have Easter egg hunts.

Rolling eggs down a slope is an ancient Easter custom that is still done in parts of Europe and the United States. On Easter Monday, children roll eggs on the lawn of the White House, the home of the president.

Above: Arriving for the Easter egg roll on the White House lawn

Right: Performing an egg dance in 17th-century Holland as a fertility rite

Eggs in the kitchen

Eggs are often used in cooking, not only for their food value, but also because of their special qualities. Egg yolks and egg whites contain protein, which hardens when it cooks. Egg white can be beaten into a foam and then cooked. As it heats up, the white hardens, trapping tiny air bubbles inside it. That is why stiffly beaten egg whites are used to make sponge cakes,

A cook in the Far East uses eggs to make special, tasty food.

soufflés, and **meringues**. The egg whites make them light and fluffy.

Egg whites are also added to ice cream. They stop the ice from becoming too hard and keep the ice cream soft and creamy.

Some food is dipped into whole beaten eggs, then into bread crumbs. The eggs make the crumbs stick to the food when it is cooked.

Egg yolks help different substances mix together, such as oil and vinegar in mayonnaise. Egg yolks are also used to thicken some soups and sauces.

How to boil an egg

You will need:

water

an egg

1. Fill a pan half-full of water and bring to a boil.

2. Using a spoon, GENTLY lower the egg into the boiling water.

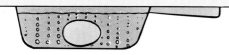

3. Boil the egg gently 3-4 minutes for a soft-boiled egg, or 10-12 minutes for a hard-boiled egg.

4. Lift the egg out with a spoon and put it in a dish. Crack the top to stop the egg from cooking.

5. Slice the top off the egg. Then eat it by scooping the cooked egg out of the shell.

26

How to fry an egg

You will need:

oil (or butter
    or margarine)
an egg

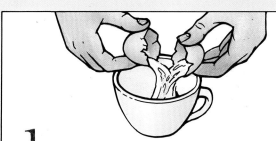

1. Break the egg into a cup.

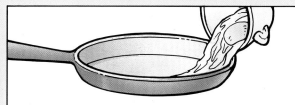

2. Heat a little oil in a frying pan, just enough to cover the bottom of the pan. When the oil is hot, carefully pour in the egg.

3. Cook the egg gently, tilting the pan and spooning the oil over the yolk to cook it completely. BE CAREFUL NOT TO SPLASH HOT OIL ON YOUR SKIN.

4. When the white is firm and the yolk is as hard or soft as you like it, lift the egg onto a plate. You might want to eat it with toast and sausage or bacon.

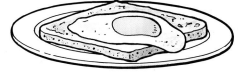

Spices and vegetables are added to scrambled eggs in this dish from southern India.

How to cook spicy scrambled eggs

You will need:

1 tablespoon butter
1 small onion, chopped
1 green chili pepper
1 small tomato, chopped
a pinch of turmeric
a pinch of salt
4 eggs, beaten with 4 tablespoons water

1. Put the butter in a nonstick pan and heat gently.

2. Add the chopped onion and fry it over low heat.

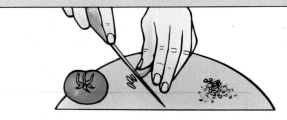

3. Remove seeds from chili pepper and chop. Add chili, tomatoes, turmeric, and salt to the pan. Stir for a minute.

4. Add the beaten eggs. Cook gently, stirring all the time, until the eggs "scramble" into smooth lumps. Serve at once.

This is a delicious, light French dessert.

How to make a sweet soufflé omelet

You will need:

3 eggs

1 tablespoon sugar

1 tablespoon butter

2-3 tablespoons jam

3. Add the whites to the yolks and stir gently, trying not to burst the tiny air bubbles in the whites.

1. Separate the eggs by cracking each one into a cup, keeping the yolk whole. Pour the white gently out of the cup into a bowl. Put the whole yolk into a second bowl.

4. Heat the butter in a frying pan. When it begins to smoke, add the egg mixture. Cook gently until the bottom of the omelet is firm.

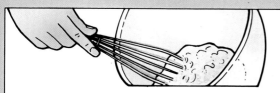

2. Using a whisk, beat the yolks with a tablespoon of sugar, and beat the whites until they are stiff.

5. Put the pan under the broiler for about a minute to cook the top of the omelet. When the top is set, spoon the jam onto the omelet.

Glossary

air sac: a space filled with air in an egg

albumen: the white of an egg

cholesterol: a fatty substance found in some foods

egg tooth: a sharp point on a chick's beak that is used to break through the eggshell

expiration date: a date that tells how long a product will be fresh

fertilized egg: an egg that contains an embryo

fowl: birds

hatch: come out of an egg

mass-produce: produce a large number or amount of something

meringue: a dessert or topping made of egg whites and sugar

mineral: a nonliving substance such as iron that our bodies need in small amounts

ovum: the egg cell from which a chick grows

protein: a substance found in such foods as eggs that is essential to human life

pullet: young hen

soufflé: a light, puffy food made with eggs

vitamin: any of a number of substances found in small amounts in food that are essential to health

yolk: the yellow part of an egg

Photo Acknowledgments

The photographs in this book were provided by: pp. 6, 9, 20, Bruce Colman/Jane Burton; p. 7 (top) Ancient Art & Architecture Collection; pp. 7 (bottom), 11, 15 (bottom), 23 (top), Wayland Picture Library; pp. 12, 14 (top and bottom), 15 (top), 22, Zefa; pp. 13, 21, 25, Christine Osborne; p. 23 (bottom), Photri.

Index

EDUCATION